PEARLY KINGDOM

BY THE SAME AUTHOR:

Town's Eye View

The London Nobody Knows

City Sights

London Overlooked

Frontispiece and Jacket
Old Montague Street, Whitechapel: the changing East End

PEARLY
KINGDOM

—— * ——

WRITTEN AND ILLUSTRATED BY

Geoffrey S. Fletcher

HUTCHINSON OF LONDON

HUTCHINSON & CO (*Publishers*) LTD

178–202 Great Portland Street London W1

London Melbourne Sydney
Auckland Bombay Toronto
Johannesburg New York

★

First published 1965

*This book has been set in Monophoto Ehrhardt, and printed in Great
Britain on Evensyde cartridge paper by William Clowes and Sons Ltd,
London and Beccles, and bound by William Brendon and Son Ltd,
Tiptree, Essex*

Contents

———— ✳ ————

Introduction

———— * ————

THIS BOOK is the product of many years' enthusiasm for and study of that vast and yet not too accurately defined city called The East End and its marginal areas. Its purpose is two-fold – to provide, as I hope, a characteristic sample of what may be discovered there, so suggesting further possibilities to the connoisseur of London, and secondly to record some carefully chosen portions of the East End before they are wiped out. Many of the subjects I had in mind originally for inclusion did, in fact, make their enforced exit while I was actually collecting material; much more will undoubtedly have gone by the time the book is published. It is true that a living city must do this, or else ossify, but the process in London in recent years has been much more than the logical one of replacement and refashioning: it has reached monstrous heights of destruction under grossly commercial ambitions on the one hand and under the arbitrary dictates of planners on the other.

The East End, extensively devastated by the war, has been further altered in character by vast rehousing developments and so called slum clearance schemes – happy homes for healthy State-controlled people, who, no doubt, would prefer to be left alone. In the process, the old closely knit life of the East End is being broken up, and is in retreat before an army of welfare workers overflowing with understanding, social observers, planners and all the sickening busybodies who flourish under the dreary conditions of post-war England. With the bureaucrats and social workers come their favourite architectural apparatus – blocks of flats, utterly at variance with the old East End, lawns that are piebald before the turves have knitted together, abstract sculpture, play areas, useless mural decorations, community centres, centres for the aged, centres for discussions – centres, in fact, for all the brain-washing the mind can conceive or compulsion execute in the worship of a classless, helpless society.

Nothing of this appears in the following pages, nothing except the frontispiece,

[9]

included as being symbolic of the new order. The old familiar monotony of seemingly endless streets, all apparently identical, is being replaced by a new monotony of giant blocks of a barrenness considerably more chilling than the old humble streets, mean as they undoubtedly were. The new East End has been resolutely ignored as being of no pictorial value whatever. It is good to know the truth, but better to know the truth and talk of palm trees.

Before proceeding further, it might be as well to attempt a definition of what exactly the East End is, geographically speaking. The area proper – what might be termed the classic East End – I always define as stretching between Bishopsgate, Aldgate and the Tower on its western boundary, up to the River Lea on its eastern, as far south as the Thames and up to Stoke Newington and Hackney Downs on the northern edge. Eighteenth-century maps show pastures and gardens in this tract of land, with occasional detached country houses. Spitalfields was built up quite early; so was Wapping and a fringe of brick and mortar advanced along the riverside to Limehouse. But the sudden expansion of industries following on the making of the docks resulted in the rapid spread of housing, and the former hamlets were joined together and largely lost their identities as the urban economy developed. That area between the City and the Lea, between Hackney and the river, was the original East London. Soon, however, the industrial explosion spread across the Lea and the isolated villages of East Ham, West Ham and Stratford were overtaken. In the last quarter of the nineteenth century, the process of absorption speeded up to take in the villages of Leyton and Walthamstow, and it still goes on. Moreover, there are parts south of the river – for instance Bermondsey and Deptford – that are as unmistakably East End as Whitechapel. Bermondsey people, when I lived there, considered themselves as authentic East Enders, and I have, therefore, included some reference to this rich area south of the river. Most of the material in this book, however, is drawn from the area we habitually, if vaguely, define as East End – between the City and Bow.

Into this vast area – and this is perhaps the most fascinating aspect of East London's history, otherwise comparatively tame – came successive waves of foreign immigrants, fleeing from religious or racial persecution or in search of a livelihood. The Jews came early, though their establishment in London life dates from their resettlement under the protection of Oliver Cromwell, largely in the eastern parts of the City and around Houndsditch. The peak period of Jewish immigration was between 1880 and the Great War, during which time about one hundred thousand settled in East London, mostly Russian and Polish Jews driven here by repressive legislation in Tsarist Russia. There were Poles in the 1830's, fleeing from the Russians, and Russian immigrants who, themselves, deemed it expedient to quit their homeland and seek the security and hospitality of London. This Russian colony, now almost obliterated, was one of the most interesting of London's alien communities up to 1914. They had their own library, bank and post office, as well as endless obscure cheap restaurants of the sort patronised by the Whitechapel murderers. In this Russian colony, Christians and Nihilists lived together, side by side with the Russian Jews. One sees them in old photographs – the Russians, peasant or educated, appearing as if from the pages of Tolstoy, with the same strange melancholy, and the Jews with the hallmark of antiquity upon them. Some of these Russians must have been integrated into the general mass of East Londoners – London has unique powers of absorption – but the virtual disappearance of such a large community after 1914 is one of the mysteries of London that I have never been able to solve.

There were the French Huguenots, the émigré nobility of the French Revolutionary period, all coming to the land of promise. The poorest of all were the children of Israel, with the fires of Joshua and Judas Maccabaeus quite gone out of their bellies. All manner of aliens went into the melting pot. The Jews arrived again in the 1930's, as well they might. There were the Irish, who came in great numbers after the potato famine, and the latest additions are those from the West Indies and West Africa.

The Chinese colony in Limehouse was dispersed during the war, but the West India Dock Road is still distinctly Oriental. There are a number of small Chinese restaurants such as the 'Old Friends', all more or less unpretentious but with excellent Chinese food. One of these is in the old house which was at one time the Chinese Mission House. Limehouse Causeway and its adjoining streets have completely altered in character. Gone are the opium rooms of the district and the Joss Houses, as far as one can tell; even the Chinese shops with their delightful inscriptions, such as 'Righteous Prosperity', belong to the past.

Most of the sweated labour of the East End in the early years of the twentieth century, when conditions were at their most frightful, was done by immigrants from Central Europe; unskilled labour most of it, in the laundering, tailoring and bootmaking trades or, indeed, anything that would keep body and soul from parting company. The almost complete disappearance of this poverty-stricken life, for ever teetering on the edge of starvation, in only a few decades is one of the most astonishing aspects of the East End – but gone it has, as a tour of the monotonous, yellow grey streets will reveal. Scarecrow children, who stare at us from old photographs, have been replaced by trim specimens in school blazers, in the very quarter where the anarchists led their shabby, furtive existence. Cars and scooters abound, and the shops are full of foods once undreamed of in Whitechapel. Pubs now cater for a well-dressed clientele, able to indulge in expensive drinks. The pub loafers, cadgers and sellers of secondhand clothes (outside the taproom on a Sunday morning) have vanished into thin air.

Even thirty years ago, conditions were still largely of a nineteenth-century character – the 1930's with their soup kitchens, bread and dripping and soleless shoes. Today's wages, with perhaps three or four in a family bringing in a total of £40 or more each week, have changed things completely, and it seems that drunkenness and wife-beating are things of the past. A good deal of gambling goes on in the East End; one sees old age pensioners tottering into betting shops – a strange sight especially in the Jack the Ripper area, where poverty was at its worst, and in Bermondsey, where something like 20,000 bets a day are placed in the betting shops. Shops are opening up almost every day in the East End for what must be one of the dullest of the vices, though many of the bookies prefer on-the-course betting.

As this poverty-haunted, pawnbroking East London has almost completely disappeared, its splendours and miseries are only to be studied in contemporary descriptions, and I recommend the reading of a few nineteenth-century accounts as an essential preliminary to East End exploration. The best way to get the feel of it as it once was is to study the books by Sir Walter Besant, who was something of a pioneer in the subject, and the reports of other early East End observers, such as Charles Booth. Some of the most revealing descriptions are by George R. Sims in his book *How the Poor Live*, which contains vivid, journalistic pictures of narrow and dirty courts full of refuse and decaying vegetable matter and squalid houses with rotting floors and damp, crumbling walls, all let out in single rooms. He gives a graphic description of an almost bare attic at the top of a rotten house and a little ragged girl of four left there without food to guard a baby all day long, while the mother was out boozing. In those days (the 1880's) marriage was not a fashionable institution in the East End, mere cohabitation without the Church's blessing being widespread, and Sims goes on to describe the plight of the families huddled in grotesque tenements by the docks and the crowds of dilapidated, hungry men waiting at the dock gates at 6 a.m., hoping to be taken on for a day's casual labour.

Still, in ridding itself of these horrors, the East End has lost its character. The baby has been emptied out with the bath water. As the poverty of the submerged is now extremely difficult to imagine, so is the boisterous life of the East End – the brightly lit gin palaces, the penny gaffs, the street markets, the noise, the gaiety of all but the most downtrodden. For them and for those without money, the principal amusement was loafing at street corners and propping up public houses. For those with money to spend, it was the pub and the music hall; the old-style free and easy held on a Monday or a Saturday night in the bar parlour or the beer-perfumed big room upstairs was dying out, killed by the halls. By the 1880's, the old sporting houses, once the resort of half the blackguards in London, especially those of the East, were also on their way out: these were the homes of boxing matches, dog fights, ratting matches and other choice diversions for 'the fancy'.

But Saturday night was the great night for the East End. Then the pubs blazed their gaslit invitations from engraved windows and bars were crammed: cheap beer, cheap gin, free clay pipes and a dazzle of light, an Impressionistic blur of faces, billycocks and barmaids, all reflected back kaleidoscopically from the rococo lettered mirrors on the walls. After the pub, the music hall – also crammed to capacity, to the ceiling above the gallery – East London was full of them. There was the Paragon in Mile End Road, where the charge for a box was but a florin, the Virgo in Pitfield Street, later renamed Harwood's Varieties, the Britannia, Hoxton (the Drury Lane of the East End), the Foresters, Cambridge Heath, the Colosseum, Dalston, and the 'Alex' in Stoke Newington – these being merely a few of the dozens of halls then open. The few that now remain are ending their days as warehouses or as a setting for all-in wrestling and bingo.

Whitechapel High Street on a Saturday night was typical. One can picture the long thoroughfare ablaze with light, the pavements crowded with bargain hunters, the kerbs with long lines of stalls and barrows – meat, fruit, fish, vegetables, poultry, cheap rabbits, cheap meat, cheap clothes, weighing chairs, try-your-strength machines, shooting galleries (prize – a genuine Whitechapel cigar), bread shops, ironmongers, penny toy shops, confectioners, lemonade and ginger beer vendors, hot potato and hokey pokey men, dealers in live animals and sellers of vividly coloured sweets. Even today iced confectionery has to be more brightly tinted in the East End than elsewhere in London. The cake shops are worth study, especially those selling the tiered iced cakes peculiar to the Jews.

Though the departing music hall has left some few desolate reminders stranded, as it were, on the mudbanks, that other celebrated institution of the Victorian East End, the gin palace, has been obliterated much more completely. Usually in London, somewhere or other at least one specimen of a type manages to survive the wreck of the years: not so the ostentatious gin palace of notorious memory. In fact, surprisingly little information has come down to us about it, and the circumstances leading to its departure and those surrounding the advent of the Victorian pub are obscure. Most of what is known about gin palaces is to be gathered from contemporary accounts as Dickens's in the *Sketches by Boz*, and drawings, often propagandist and hostile, by artists such as Cruickshank; the pictorial records, however, are slight and inconclusive. Briefly, a gin palace had these characteristics: a long bar, backed with large barrels, lavish decoration, impressive gas fittings and so on – and, of course, tarty barmaids made to measure: the whole generally rakish: and an exterior with plenty of corrupt, flashy, 'Grecian' ornament, an imposing no-expense-spared entrance, an illuminated clock and other devices calculated to bait the customers in from frowzy basement and unlovely street. The heyday of the gin palace was roughly from 1830 to 1860, generally speaking, and the transition (if indeed there was one) to the fruity Victorian pub we still appreciate, with its centrally placed bar fitting and various bars of varying degrees of elaboration and comfort radiating from it, but screened from one another, is not properly understood.

I am, I believe, absolutely correct in stating that not a single gin palace remains in the East End today, or the rest of London for that matter, the delightful Henekey's in Holborn being the only one approximating to the gin palace of the early and mid-nineteenth century. Lock, stock and barrel, the gin palace has gone. However, in years of East End wandering, I have found intriguing traces, though maddeningly fragmentary, of that once flourishing institution. There is a pub near Leman Street, going west to Tower Hill, which shows every sign in its superstructure of once being a gin palace, remodelled on the ground floor by the later Victorians and turned into a pub, and in Narrow Street, Limehouse, on a corner site opposite to the Causeway, is a florid, late Regency building (gin palaces were nearly always corner sited) of c. 1830, once called 'The Distillery'. It functioned as a pub up to a quarter of a century ago, but its style, details and size are those of pure gin palace architecture, which is what I believe it to have been. There may be one or two others in the East End, and I can think of no programme more intriguing than a search for them, based on a study of contemporary descriptions and illustrations.

In fact, the East End offers unequalled opportunities for rewarding exploration. The bus routes going east from Aldgate make it easy, but nothing has yet been devised, the bicycle excepted, to supersede the human legs when knowledge and experience of great cities is sought after; if the feet are not up to it, why then, those little corner shops that abound in the East End are prepared to sell you corn paste from a marvellous card with Union Jacks on top, nor are certain Professors skilled in ailments of the feet entirely lacking in the market places. Only recently I discovered one of my favourite quacks of years ago still in practice. His corn solvent was selling as well as ever, its qualities having apparently not diminished since Queen Mary wrote her enthusiastic approval, testifying to the wonderful effect it had on her feet and adding that a box ought to be in the possession of each of her subjects. Even on Bank Holidays, the East Londoner was not deprived of his foot comforts, for the pedlars of patent medicines, in spite of being under Royal Patronage, were not above following the trade winds to Hampstead and other open spaces where their clients were wont to gather.

No doubt the shortage of hotel accommodation has prevented some otherwise enterprising travel agent from organising holidays in the East End, but the novelty of a week in that dim and disappearing region would surely be a refreshing change from those same tourist-haunted places that occur with depressing monotony in the glossy brochures. I should do the thing thoroughly, giving my clients an intriguing, unforgettable holiday, based on a doss house where the guests would be accommodated. Tours of Peabody flats, Working Men's Hostels and Improved Dwellings would be on the itinerary, and meals would be taken at a selection of Yiddish restaurants, stewed eel shops, cheap caffs, coffee stalls and the like. Docks, warehouses and former music halls would add to the delights, together with pubs and betting shops. One of the highlights would be a visit to the Abbey Mills Pumping Station illustrated on page 27. Optional extras are a feature of most good packaged holidays; those in mine would include visits to mildewy church halls, the Jack the Ripper area (with a decayed old man who remembered the scare signing photographs), a day in Cable Street and a leisurely inspection of the remaining Victorian lavatories, with time allowed for photography.

Another marked change is the total disappearance of the costermongering class – those who went with the donkey and cart to Chingford or Epping on Bank Holidays if in funds or else (all too often after a succession of wet Saturdays) took the same donkey and cart to the Caledonian Market and went out of business.

The Parisian midinette I believe to be a romantic fiction, created by the imagination of Murger and such, but the East End factory girl was real enough and existed once as a distinct type – Board School educated, a few years at a jam factory, early marriage *et sequentia*. She had a healthy, if raw, complexion, good enough looks that deteriorated shortly after marriage, blue striped apron and a homely code – new clothes on Bank Holidays and at 16 or 17 a factory sweetheart. Mean Street, for she settled near her parents after the wedding, was the whole of her life – a perspective of yellow houses, a horizon of chimney pots. She taught her children the things she herself had learned, skimped, saved and shopped. The children grew up and repeated the process, and the raw cemetery claimed her at last, after an East End funeral. What did it all mean?

Her present-day descendant is impatient of all restrictions, and has money to spend. At first glance, and sometimes hardly at all, she differs little from girls in other parts of London. She goes up West and very likely works there, and could not be satisfied with a field day at Epping, organised by the ladies of a church, with lemonade and buns and a little prayer of thanks to follow. She is dead beat often enough, transistorised, prepackaged, buys the top pop records as fast as they come out, likes to show her legs and knows neither buns nor Jesus. Perhaps, after all, the ladies of the church were wrong. If so, their stodginess ought to be forgiven; living in such dark days, they could not see the coming brightness of the mid-twentieth century, nor had its screaming reached their ears.

The disappearance of the pawnbrokers is another symptom of absolute change, and the free dispensaries – though the gloomy doctors' surgeries of the meaner quarters (just an ordinary shop turned into a waiting room) are still plentiful.

Pawnbrokers are almost as rare a sight now as East End street fights or the bare-foot brigade. There were hundreds of pawnbrokers in the East End at the turn of the century, ministering to the needy whose ever-recurring wants in the way of spot cash could be accommodated in exchange for the pledging of articles of clothing, bedding and furniture, usually redeemed on Saturday nights unless permanent financial embarrassment sent one's belongings up the spout for ever.

Amid so much alteration, one custom of the East Londoner remains apparently unaffected by time and change – the habit of consuming shellfish and jellied eels. The oyster stalls have disappeared, oysters being no longer the cheap article they were in the last century. But the economical, long-lasting (because at times rub-bery) whelk retains its hold, together with the humble winkle, cockle and succul-ent mussel. The taste for these dainties seems to have been passed on to the younger generation who patronise the shellfish stalls outside the East End pubs on a Saturday night. These stalls, no longer lit by flaring naphtha lamps, add a picturesque touch to those pubs not architecturally notable, such as the 'City Arms', Millwall, and the 'Gregorian Arms' on the Jamaica Road. Bearing in mind the popularity of shellfish, I am always forcibly struck by the solemn, even indif-ferent, way in which Londoners consume them, without registering any emotion, as if assisting at some religious rite in which they entirely disbelieved. Abroad, the Dutchman beams as he swallows whole a succession of little sardine-like fish in the streets of Amsterdam, and the Frenchman eyes his dish of hot mussels, bottle of red wine and roll with a connoisseur's relish. Not so the East Ender, who gazes into the darkness from the brilliantly lit stall out of weary eyes, absorbing the contents of the little dish with an apathy wonderful to see. The same low-spiritedness is to be found in the jellied and stewed eel shops, the mirrors of which reflect a collection of lined and careworn faces, eating, as it would appear, from compulsion, with infinite sadness and gloom. I cannot believe that this settled moroseness is anything more than a trend of the last few decades. In the bad old days of chronic overcrowding in a vast slum area, where visits to 'Uncle' and the midnight flit with one's possessions heaped on a barrow were regular features of the struggle for existence, the East Ender had at least his moments of hilarity. I have mentioned the Saturday nights in Whitechapel as an instance; the Bank Holidays were another, and one imagines the joy of an evening at a melo-drama at such places as the Britannia in Hoxton or an evening at the Queen's, Poplar, after preliminaries at Charlie Brown's. The Britannia audiences were partial to hot pies and peas during the performance: you bought your pie, bit a hole in it and the pieman poured the gravy in from a can. For Sunday, there was the richness of Petticoat Lane and its tributaries – Sclater Street and its bird market, Cutler Street and Brick Lane; lemonade, gherkins, fish, flash clothes, secondhand clothes, fruit, toys, indestructible boots, warranted watches and

[16]

chains; bearded Jews, men with drooping moustaches under cloth caps and a babble of cockney and foreign voices. Petticoat Lane, officially Middlesex Street since the late 1840's, has no longer the same vitality and diversity, interesting though it still remains. This individuality and liveliness is being gradually eliminated from the East End. That is why those who intend to see it should do so now before all becomes as dull as ditchwater or Lansbury. Sample stewed eels and mash, therefore, survey the East End from a box in an old-fashioned dining-room or from behind a paper full of fish and chips in the street, explore the vanishing world of endless streets and little shops, seeking out those disappearing types of Cockneydom who required Dickens and Phil May, Albert Chevalier and George Belcher to do them justice.

For those unable to study the changing East End at leisure, a single afternoon spent in the neighbourhood of Aldgate will yield a comprehensive sample of the whole. There are the two ancient houses (one a pub) on the south side of Aldgate High Street, the only remaining ones of an extensive row, once inhabited by butchers. From here there is Leman Street with Alie Street branching off, Cable Street and Wellclose Square. North of Aldgate is Wentworth Street and Brick Lane and that most crumbling, truly representative East End street already mentioned, Old Montague Street. This is a street for the East End fancier and no mistake – though not for long, the entire area being marked down for demolition. Besides the herring shop, drawn on pages 31 and 33, there is a variety of little mixed businesses, a Jewish bookseller and several Jewish confectioners. Indian and Pakistani sweetmeat shops rub shoulders with obscure little restaurants and greengrocers, whose richly coloured offerings spill over the pavements in bags and boxes. There are enough greasy tenement houses here and in Greatorex Street to satisfy even the most fastidious, and a unique collection of poor immi-grants, ancient Jews and frowzy whites, punctuated with an occasional honest Cockney face, sometimes on top of an old, tottering body engaged in shoving laundry or stooping between heavy bags. As in Cable Street, the frowzy property seems in imminent danger of collapse. Kids of all nations, Jew and Gentile, plain and coloured, strong or starved, swarm everywhere, and tired men lounge against the iron posts with which the street has been liberally furnished. The frontispiece to this book conveys the mood exactly – rotting old houses with modern flats (the shape of things to come) looming above and a foreground of strange beings – in this case, a blind old man led by a little girl, an old clo' man with his pram and coloured men talking to blondes. Up and down the street on each side, heads stick out of windows, elbows on sills, the whole perfumed by a rich fragrance com-pounded of unwashed humanity and strongly scented delicacies from the Eastern cook-shops. The whole can be studied in the course of an hour or so.

The destruction of the Columbia Market, supreme among all Gothic fantasies

2

[17]

in London, was an irreparable loss to the East End; it represented the triumph of romance over experience. The costers never quite cottoned on to it, preferring to keep the donkey in the back-yard and, frequently, their stock-in-trade in their own living quarters. These vegetables were usually revived at the water butt which served the entire alley: thus it was that the costers of the Victorian age carried the contagious diseases of the East End to the better-class districts and suburbs; too often an unwelcome customer, whose decision was final, accompanied the donkey and cart. Though the Columbia Market has gone, there are many remaining specimens of Victorian Gothic in East London forming a special subject of study, very eloquent of a vanished idealistic philanthropy that can be recaptured on occasion when the mood and circumstances are right with surprising vividness and pathos.

The mention of Columbia Market and its adjoining Gothic dwellings brings me to another characteristic feature of the East End offering abundant historical interest – those great blocks of improved or model dwellings. Bethnal Green is a good place to study the early working class housing by which the Victorians sought to ameliorate the overcrowded conditions of London's prime slum area and to reform its formidable despair. These early blocks of the 1850's and 1860's are supremely lowering to the mind with their open iron galleries and barrack-like elevations. In fact, they are considerably more depressing than the cottages they were designed to supersede. Most of the Waterlow or Peabody blocks are in a vaguely Italianate manner, but the L.C.C. in the Boundary Street estate and other early rehousing schemes adopted its own style, even more unfeeling than the work of Norman Shaw to which it seems dimly related. Other early blocks of artisans' flats remain intact in the Spitalfields area, and there is a choice block of Gothic dwellings in Wentworth Street, adjoining Toynbee Hall, dating from the 1880's. The great impediment to a full appreciation of all these gloomy Victorian 'dwellings' is that the industrious classes for whom they were originally designed have vanished; the architecture and the people are no longer in unison. A distant view is tolerable enough, but at close range the want of harmony between those gaunt open staircases with lavatories and water taps, those deeply recessed windows, that heavy-handed detailing is painfully felt: you look for paper-capped carpenters, ragged urchins, rough fellows and fighting women and find only tarty blondes, loose-limbed, velvet-collared youths and the comfortable middle aged.

You look for the terraced houses where families lived for generations, the whole outfit revolving round the ubiquitous, majestic Ma, you want the anonymous houses with scraps of garden where nothing ever grew and you look for the little cottages down dark courtyards, where the tin bath hung on the scullery wall, awaiting the Saturday night ablutions. But it is all going. You find yourself among neighbourhood units, comprehensive development areas, multi-storey blocks, a new uniformity more frightful than the old. Often, you cannot recognise the old landmarks and feel the conviction coming strong upon you that the only thing to do with a neighbourhood unit is to get as far away from it as possible. Old slave-driver employer, new impertinent bureaucrat. Old-time evangelist with buns and Heaven, new-style welfare worker with Hell and orange juice. Pictures of the Queen are less frequently encountered nowadays, and framed certificates of friendly societies are no longer prized as decorations. Bibles, aspidistras and plaster alsatians are a drug on the market. In fact, the East End is altering more quickly than the West End, but its changes receive less publicity. I hope the following pages will be acceptable as at least a reflection, however inadequate, of its former richness and individuality.

The Drawings

———— ✳ ————

I

Garden in the New Kent Road

———— * ————

I NEVER pass this wonderful mixture of gardening and popular art without thinking of Gus Elen's song about the very pretty garden that was pleasant on a summer afternoon – the coster's backyard decorated with turnip tops – and its view of the Crystal Palace, spoiled only by the 'ouses in between. What strikes the eye in this garden, after the heliotrope paintwork, is the extraordinary quantity of thriving plants, crammed into the beds among statues of dogs, cherry boys and the like, and the intermingling of real and artificial flowers. The angry-looking stork rising from an aspidistra is one of those frequently encountered in the little London dairies once upon a time: he is, therefore, quite at home in the New Kent Road. The bed on the right of the drawing is a mass of pansies, delphiniums and purple lupins: dogs and a Grecian figure peer from the leaves. Hanging baskets of outsize plastic roses are disposed about the area railings and the steps are guarded by an armoured knight. There are plenty of shells (no garden of this kind being complete without them) and an assortment of rustic benches and pergolas.

These fine eighteenth-century houses of the New and Old Kent Roads reached their lowest ebb in the years of unemployment before the last war. With the Welfare State they have been tarted up to some extent; the brickwork is grimy still, but the paint is constantly renewed, often in surprising colours. Local pubs have also had an interior uplift.

Garden in the
New Kent Road

2

Limehouse Lock

———————— ✳ ————————

TYPICAL OF the industrial landscapes of the dock areas of the East End – nothing architecturally remarkable but offering interesting, stimulating shapes – in this case the curving bridge and worn brickwork of the warehouses behind, with a decorative touch supplied by the lamp. Here, in the lockside cafe, you can indulge in a cup of hot sweet tea and a thick ham sandwich and watch the timber-laden barges entering the lock, for there is much traffic at high tide. The other part of the lock, extremely pictorial, is reproduced on page 83.

3

Byzantine Sewage Station
Abbey Mills

———— * ————

ONLY THE Victorians had the supreme confidence to erect sewage works in the grand manner, of cathedral-like proportions and rich with cast iron. Abbey Mills is one of the rarest joys of the East End. You approach it down a dreary road from a point beyond Bow, and suddenly come upon a park where strange towers and cupolas of grey and coloured brick appear between the trees. I took care to choose a day of wind, rain and grey, shapeless cloud for my visit in order to contrive the utmost harmony; leaves were circling round in an autumn dance of death and late chrysanthemums were flowering.

Abbey Mills Pumping Station was constructed between 1865 and 1868 as part of Sir Joseph Bazalgette's scheme for the main drainage of London. The two Northern Low Level Sewers and the Isle of Dogs Branch Sewer meet at the station and the sewage and part of the storm water from the Low Level system is lifted about 40′ 0″ to the Outfall sewers, which lie in the embankment on the north-east side of the station, in which the flow gravitates to the Northern Outfall Works, some four miles distant. The low level area of North London from which all dry-weather flow is pumped to the Northern Outfall Sewers at Abbey Mills covers in all about 45 square miles. Approximately 23 square miles of this is in Hammersmith, Fulham, Chelsea, Kensington, Westminster, Holborn, Finsbury, Shoreditch, Bethnal Green, Stepney and Poplar, and $21\frac{1}{2}$ square miles outside the County, comprising the Boroughs of Acton, Tottenham and Wood Green, Leyton and Walthamstow.

The main engine house was built between 1865 and 1868 and originally housed eight beam engines of a gross capacity of about 112,000 gallons a minute. These sets were removed in stages between 1931 and 1933 and replaced by eight electrically driven centrifugal pumps. Fortunately the newer installations do not seriously disrupt the nineteenth-century atmosphere. The box-like office between the pillars might be a pulpit – for a sanitary inspector's sermon.

Abbey Mills
Sewage Pumping
Station

4

Charlie's with the Green Winders
Pownall Terrace, Kennington

——————— ✳ ———————

POWNALL TERRACE is typical of the many decently proportioned, second-rate terraces of the East End, nearly always run up by speculative builders who named them after themselves or members of their families or after some national victory or hero, such as Nelson or Trafalgar. Sometimes the appeal was to Royal associations – Brunswick or Hanover occasionally – reaching the summit of aspiration with Belle Vue, Elysium or Paradise (usually in flat contradiction to the facts). The house with the corrugated iron at the door and ground-floor window was one of the early homes of the immortal Charles Chaplin. Today the houses are at an advanced stage of decay. Most of the terrace is untenanted and is soon to be demolished. Few locals seemed to know that the distinguished Charlie had been a neighbour, but one little girl, playing in the mud in true East End fashion, pointed out the house to me, saying, 'That's Charlie's, mister, Charlie's with the green winders – but he don't live there any more.'

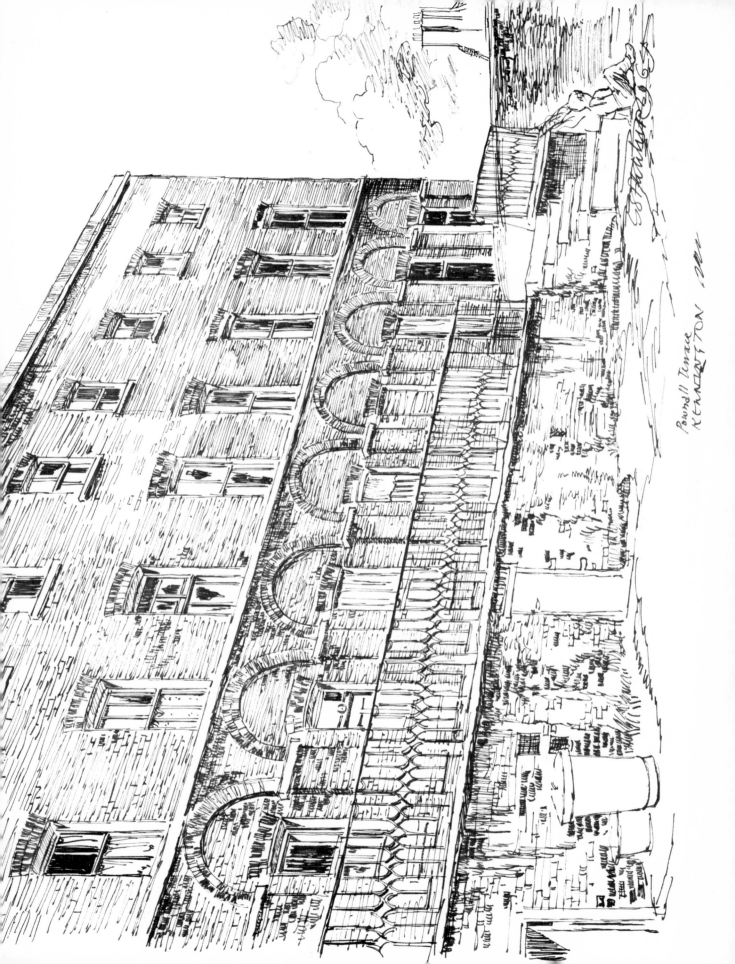

Burdall Terrace
KENNINGTON

5

Herring Shop, Frostic Place

———— * ————

IN OLD MONTAGUE STREET, a street to be visited again and again by those in search of the genuine vintage East End. There is not much time left in which to do it, for the area is to be demolished, and the frontispiece to this book shows what has already happened to the opposite end of Old Montague Street, as well as symbolising in a dramatic way the destruction of the East End as a whole. Meantime, the old Jewess with shawl and ivory cameo carries on conversations with passers-by from the dark interior of her shop, for the establishment is open to the street on one side and shuttered on the other. It reminds me of certain old shops in the area of Les Halles, the whole thing being in fact reminiscent of Whistler's etching of the mustard seller. There are glass tanks full of pickled cucumbers – a favourite dainty with the locals – odoriferous barrels of herrings, a sanded floor and a black cat. The interior, with the owner, appears in the drawing on the next page. Outside the shop passes a constant procession of Asiatics, ancient Jews, old shuffling women, half crazy old men, strutting pigeons and leaking dogs.

Herring Shop
Frostic Place.

6

The Pickled Herring Seller

———————— ✳ ————————

'SO YOU want to take my portrait? I'm not young and attractive any longer. Everything's changed. This part was once a Ghetto, but there's not so many Jewish people here now and few of those keep up the old customs. Most of my customers are Jewish or Polish. They eat the pickled cucumbers with bread and butter. But I like art. So does the Queen. She's got lots of pictures at home at the Palace. I once saw the Kaiser's palace at Potsdam – there was a room studded with diamonds – would you believe that? – and the Kaiserina buried her dogs in the garden. There's lots of West Indians here now, same as in Stoke Newington, where Jews as well as Gentiles are moving out. They won't stay. My black cat is supposed to be lucky but he isn't. He's a naughty boy. Everything's changed. . . .'

7

Obelisk in Limehouse Churchyard

————————— ∗ —————————

THIS DRAMATIC, eighteenth-century, pyramidal tomb combines admirably with the Roman grandeur of Hawksmore's church of St. Anne. The drawing was made on a day of intense thundery heat with the sun like a brass gong in a sky of livid pink, against which the dark green leaves of the aspens fluttered wildly, beckoning the storm. There was the same brooding atmosphere as in a landscape by Poussin. The Portland stone pyramid is grimly bound with iron cramps. Its surface is so pitted that the inscription is indecipherable, though a date, December 1790, can be made out near the base. There is also a decayed coat of arms and, above, in the apex of the monument, the words 'The Wisdom of Solomon Chapter . . .', the rest being obliterated by time and weather.

Obelisk in
Limehouse Churchyard

8

The 'Grapes', Limehouse

———— ✳ ————

THE ORIGINAL of the 'Six Jolly Fellowship Porters' in *Our Mutual Friend* and one of the most attractive, because unspoiled, riverside pubs. The 'Grapes' has a wainscoted public bar, yellow grained in the good old style, a piano topped by a jug of flowers and a telly on the wall. There are hardly any improvements, and the customers are almost entirely locals. Approach it down Three Colt Lane, a twisty street of small shops (where a Jewish cobbler once tried to sell me his business as a going concern for £800) leading to Narrow Street and a group of eighteenth-century buildings, most of them now empty, adjoining the 'Grapes'. These were once the premises of ship and barge builders, who lived above their workshops and wharves. Once when painting the 'Grapes' in winter time from a barge moored in the river, I discovered that the tide had floated me well out and the return journey, loaded with tackle, across slippery narrow planks was by no means comforting – especially the last forty feet or so over open, swirling river. The reward for a safe landing was tea and crumpets round the fire at the barge builders. The old houses adjoining the 'Grapes' are marked down for demolition.

The Grapes, Limehouse

9

The Classic Ruins of Bermondsey:
St. John's, Horselydown

——————— ∗ ———————

BUILT IN 1732. The architect is unknown but possibly John James or Samuel Tufnell. It had a curious spire in the shape of a column, now entirely disappeared. The church, of which only three outer walls survive from the war-time destruction, is also to go, along with the Rectory, a plain mid–eighteenth-century building with some good panelling and a graceful staircase. The ruined church, overgrown with elder and other shrubs, presents a Piranesi–like appearance, very much at variance with its surroundings.

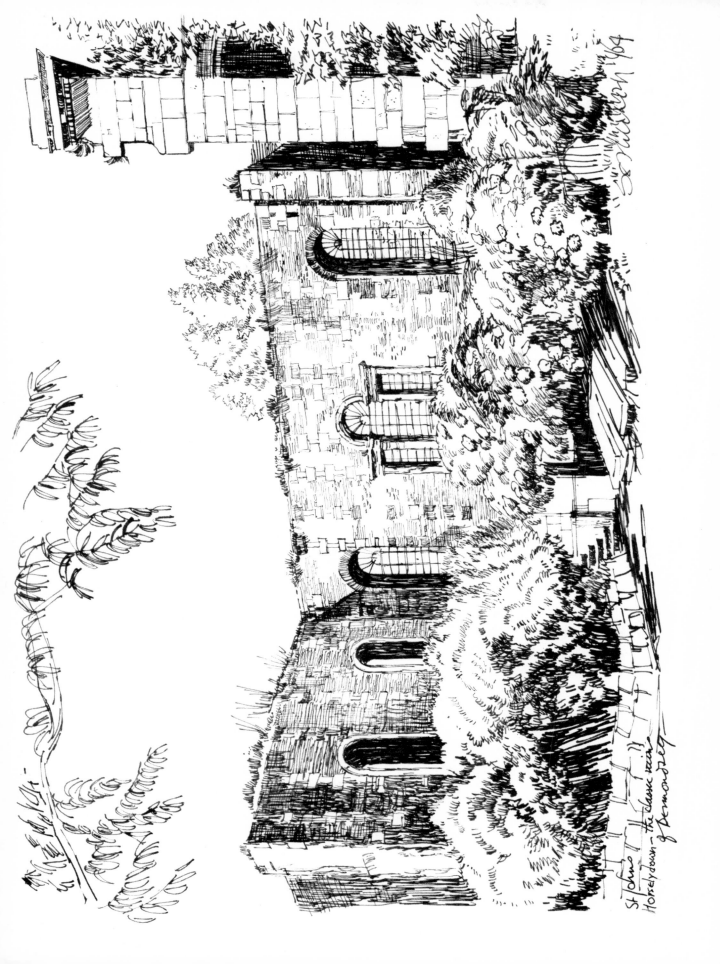

St John's
Horselydown — the classic house
J Desmond [?]

IO

High Street, West Ham
Saturday Afternoon

———————— ✳ ————————

IN THE background, an Edwardian billiard hall, the last flowering of English Baroque. In the foreground, a seemingly endless procession of prams – one could hardly believe so many infants could be fitted into the teeming East End. Judging by the condition of many of the women, the supply seems likely to continue un-abated. You cannot escape from the Salvation Army for long in the East End – you might as well try to escape from God. Their band sets up and plays by the Town Hall, resounding above the traffic, yelling kids and the noises of the street market. A group of chewing youths form a half-circle round the band, applauding when the hymn is over. Two clean-shaven warriors unfold a rare document from a briefcase, holding it before the crowd. It proves to be a huge cheque, dated Heaven, 11th November 1963: The Bank of Heaven will pay Eternal Life to whomsoever believeth – signed, the Word of God. But above the group is a banner on the Town Hall announcing a Sunday jiving session – the World, the Flesh and the Devil!

An old man plays a curious instrument in the gutter outside Woolworth's; coaxing an infinitely pathetic melody – a broken melody – from a wire stretched across a plank. His arms are tattooed, he has no socks and his shoes are heading for the last round-up.

The shipyards of the Thames Ironworks Company at West Ham were among the most important of the Victorian age. They built H.M.S. *Warrior*, the first Ironclad, in 1860, and the company's football team became West Ham United.

11

Alie Street

———————— ❋ ————————

BEHIND AND to the south of Aldgate, a street of chronically dilapidated eighteenth-century houses, one of which had, until recently, a fine carved doorway
with foliage and heads of cherubs of the type found in Deptford. I intended to
record it in this book, but it had been destroyed between my visits. The group in
the drawing, also eighteenth century, are in a pleasing state of decay – brickwork
black and furred with dirt, windows leaning this way and that. White men are
rarities here nowadays, the area being full of coloured immigrants, whose warm,
overpowering smell contends with that of spices and the effluvia from over-
tenanted houses. There is a synagogue of 1894 (or, if you prefer it, 5654) and a
nice old pub, the 'White Swan', which retains its ornamental Victorian bracket,
though no longer supporting a lamp. There is a charming tiled picture of a swan
and overhanging tree in pale green and white, all of a Walter Crane flavour.

HALF MOON PASSAGE E

B.OGAZI

Alie Street

12

George Carter & Sons
Old Kent Road

———————— ✳ ————————

THIS SPLENDID stuccoed store is one of the few surviving examples of the large London emporium of the mid-Victorian age, appearing very much as they all did at the time of their début: classic details, stuccoed finery, homely grandeur. Most of the West End stores – Harrods, for instance – started in a similar architectural style. George Carter's classic equipment includes female heads in the Victorian Grecian of the Great Exhibition, male heads of the Corn Law period, lions and curlicue brackets. But those mural decorations of cupids with straw-coloured hair and a little wispy something at their waists, all at sea – three of them to a waterproof titfer – what could be more enchanting? Nothing, surely, except the gent below whose walrus moustache dispiritedly droops beneath his 'coke'. And no wonder, for the poor guy sports a clock face just where his belly ought to be, and is, no doubt, uncomfortably aware of being pure Salvador Dali.

13

Rummage Sale, Deptford

———— ＊ ————

RUMMAGE OR jumble sale – the terms are interchangeable. Each, being interpreted, means the same – a death-defying scramble for old clothes and footwear that can hardly stand another turn on London pavements, monstrous ornaments, a miscellaneous mass of literature and, in fine, down-and-out versions of almost every article the human soul has ever coveted in its earthly pilgrimage. Jumble sales are best when held in peeling church halls, full of deal cupboards and musty old prayer books, especially if refreshments are served – tea in thick cups and slices of cake of the kind once known as 'tram-stoppers'. Such events are often announced in transcendental terms closely resembling those of showmen, 'Great' or 'Grand' being about the most modest, with 'Colossal' at the upper end of the scale.

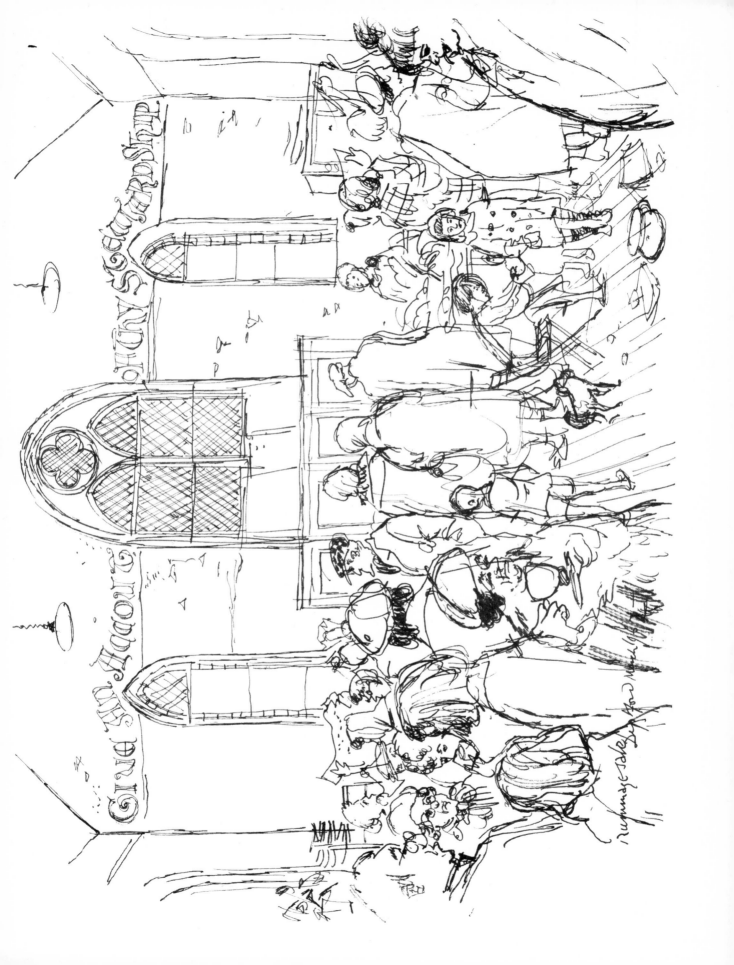

14

The Ruins of the Parthenon
Greenwich

———————— ✳ ————————

IT IS suitable that a neighbourhood rich in classically inspired architecture should have its ruined Parthenon, even if only a music hall. The Parthenon, which passed through the usual transformation to become a cinema, was originally known as Crowder's, so called after its owner C. S. Crowder who opened it on 28th October 1871. The derelict auditorium is of bijou proportions, with a stage to match. Much of the charming fibrous plaster decorations remain, and the proscenium arch is all but intact. Today the place is used as a store for scenery and 'props'. Its heyday coincided with that of Greenwich as a place of resort for the East Londoner on those Bank Holiday afternoons of shrimps and watercress, sherbet and ginger beer, winkles and whelks, when the route from Greenwich Pier to the Park was lined with stalls and hucksters of every conceivable sort and the beer flowed free and cheap. By the time this book is published, the work of turning the Parthenon into the new Greenwich Theatre will have begun. The old proscenium arch is to be retained, but the gallery, one of the steepest in London, is decayed beyond redemption.

Parthenon
music Hall Greenwich

15

Street Market, Whitechapel

———————— * ————————

WHITECHAPEL HIGH STREET is unusually wide, the reason being that the great Whitechapel Hay Market occupied the centre of the road for generations, the tram company being obliged to lay their tracks on either side of it. Now the horse has almost departed and trees, monument and stalls give a deceptively Parisian air to matter-of-fact Cockneydom. The foreground figures give the show away; they belong exclusively to the East End. Signs of poverty have disappeared, along with horses, fodder and trams, or only appear in isolation – smelly old men in clothes originally made for somebody else, trousers at half mast, Casey Court boots. Instead come convoys of gleaming prams, girls with huge heads of bouffé hair, iridescently tinted and with a texture like candy floss, and beaming pink infants. The money and the transistor music goes round and round. The monument is to Edward VII, erected by the Jews of East London.

Whitechapel.

16

Eighteenth-Century Doorway
Elder Street, Spitalfields

————— * —————

SPITALFIELDS IS one of the most fascinating parts of the East End, its special qualities stemming from the slum life of the area and the decayed splendour of its architecture. Elder Street has a selection of fine doorways on the opposite side of the street to the one illustrated, two having rusticated pilasters supporting a frieze and cornice. In another the metopes are filled with carved rosettes entirely occupying the square. Even the area railings, in a flattened S-shaped curve, are eloquent of the beauty and sensibility of eighteenth–century domestic architecture. It all reminds us of the prosperity of Spitalfields in the mid–eighteenth century. In the Victorian age, this quarter of London degenerated to indescribable depths of poverty and inertia. Whole families herded themselves together in single rooms. There was often no money to pay for the funerals and a bereaved family would, therefore, keep the corpse in the same room in which they lived, ate and slept. There were instances of dead children being kept for as long as fifteen days, uncoffined, decomposing and offensive. Old men and women were similarly allowed to remain unburied, either in the living room or bundled into a shed in the yard, until the parish authorities stepped in and paid for the funeral.

S S Paldehll
Elder Street
Spitalfields.

17

Jellied Eel and Whelk Stalls, Aldgate

———————— ✳ ————————

CHAUCER LIVED in Aldgate, quite literally, for he occupied rooms about the gateway. I have often considered, when wandering round this fruity quarter, whether its habit of consuming jellied eels and shellfish from stalls in the street goes back to the poet's time. The City stops dead at Aldgate pump. After it comes the quick, stimulating transition to that whelk-and-fruit-flavoured, flashy tract of land where the East End commences.

One of my favourite thoroughfares about here is Leman Street, a sunless, gloomy street where, passing between the great C.W.S. warehouses of various periods, one feels suddenly transported to Manchester. Leman Street is one of the few London streets where horse droppings are still seen, and there is the Manor House hostel, a working man's home, an eighteenth-century town house now completely derelict, and the late nineteenth-century police station associated with the investigations into the Houndsditch murders and the affair in Sidney Street.

No WAITING

TUBBY ISA

TUBBY ISAACS
ALDGATE

TUBBY ISAACS
ALDGATE

TUBBY ISAAC
ALDGATE

GSFletcher
Aldgate - jellied &
whelk stalls

18

Old Houses, Rotherhithe Street

———— * ————

AN EXAMPLE of what the old riverside architecture of the East End once was. This curious and interesting old collection (with my own house, 'The Little Midshipman', on the extreme right) has now been demolished, so I have included the drawing as a record. Braithwaite and Dean's (once an oar-maker's) on the left of the drawing now stands in splendid isolation, adjoining the stupid riverside garden made by the L.C.C. Opposite this garden was a row of bow-fronted shops, including a twine dealer's and a dairy; war damage closed their account. Next to the Little Midshipman was Yardley's Wharf, also a war casualty, and Cochin's pepper and spice mill. A market was held in Rotherhithe Street in the nineteenth century. Bermondsey was full of quaint houses until comparatively recent times, a token of its desirability as a place of residence at a former period. Bridge House in George Row, Dockhead, was typical of these, an old house with panelled rooms and a well in the garden. Pocock's, the barge builders, the tall brick house next to the 'Jolly Waterman' in the drawing, was another, possessing a fine staircase with barley sugar columns. It was a sad business, making this drawing, for the houses were all too obviously awaiting their vandalistic demolition at the time. A faded Union Jack, contemporary type of all that is vain and outmoded, fluttered pitifully from one of the walls.

19

Fruit Stalls, Hackney

———— ✳ ————

HACKNEY, ON the northern edges of the East End, is rich in material for the East End fancier. In its main street, near the medieval church tower, a dental surgeon occupies eighteenth-century premises that have the look of having once been a chop house (it is almost worth while being plagued with toothache in order to have one's molars extracted in such an architectural framework) and there are some choice opticians' signs hanging over the pavement (the kind that have a pair of naturalistic eyes set in spectacles) and some fine Victorian pubs, the 'Crown', for instance, at the junction of Dalston Lane, with its projecting canopy supported by cast-iron columns painted in imitation of marble. Only a dedicated pavement artist would have attempted the subject opposite, for the traffic jams occurring every few minutes and the heat and dust made drawing a burden. Even so, the scent of fruit and vegetables wafted across the road; perhaps this scent attracted the butterfly I noticed making a hazardous and fortunately successful crossing between the traffic. As I drew, a magnificent East End funeral passed. The hearse was stuffed with flowers, including a vast 'floral tribute' composed of red roses with the inscription 'To Dad, the best friend in the world' in huge silver letters. There followed a formidable turn-out of the family, mainly red-eyed females with hooked noses and idiotic red-faced youths, Uncle Pentstemon and Polly to the life, sweating under a celluloid collar.

20

Victorian Veterinary Surgeon's
Bermondsey

———— * ————

YOU CAN still hear the jingle of harness and steady clip-clop of horses' hooves in the spicy-smelling streets of Bermondsey, but this splendid nineteenth-century vet's and forge at the corner of Morocco Street has been closed for over a decade. Once the big doors were open all day, with lines of horses in front, waiting to be shod. Local people collected manure from the four-footed clients who supplied it gratis while awaiting their turn. The façade is in white glazed brick with bands of pale blue and mouldings and inset panels of yellow glazed terra-cotta. There were two heads of horses above the ground-floor doors; only one remains now and the moulded work is much decayed in places, particularly on the cornice. But the whole thing is quite splendid and one of the finest examples known to me from the great days of the patient, intelligent horse, whose sufferings, especially in the shafts of buses, must have been almost indescribable. It is typical of man that he should treat a creature so obviously his superior to such abominable servitude. Note the decorative ironwork in the ventilators above the door. Period, early 'nineties or sometime during the previous decade, but 1880 in feeling.

Victorian Vets
Bermondsey

21

Theatre Royal, Stratford

——————— * ———————

THE DULL exterior gives no hint whatever of the charming interior arrangements of what is one of the prettiest auditoriums in London, and the Theatre Royal has a Victorian bar to add to its pleasures. The delicacy of the interior is in strong contrast to Angel Lane outside. This is a huddle of old, low houses and shops, including a period café with marble-topped tables, mirrors and glass jars that must have once contained Abernethy biscuits. Several of these low-browed old shops still have their late Victorian white glass lamps outside. The fish shops are very picturesque, Cohen's fish and chip shop being perhaps the best, with its white tiles and Art Nouveau lettering and ornament.

Theatre Royal Stratford

22

Pavement Antiques, Whitechapel

———— ∗ ————

ONE OF those suddenly conceived, rapidly but vaguely executed displays of junk common to the East End; a small quick profit being taken for a one-hour stand. A pram, long past retiring age, provides the transport. From it, the two merchant adventurers unload plastic beakers, galvanised buckets, odds and ends of rusty old tools and salvaged stock of all sorts. Popular art is represented by a pile of false teeth, the taboos that have no name by damaged enamel jerries, culture by superannuated gramophone records. As always in London, eminently so in the East End, a crowd quickly gathers. It melts as rapidly, the two business partners retiring to split their profit in the lavatory under the plane trees.

Pavement Antique
Whitechapel

23

Summer Evening in Clarence Place
Hackney

——————————— * ———————————

HACKNEY, NOT, as in the music-hall song, with the 'ouses took away, but with them delightfully left in, and very appealing – though as yet unfashionable – on a summer evening under the shadows of the lime and chestnut trees. Clapton Square is green and well planted with shapely trees. Dignified, shabby, terraced houses remain on two sides. Clarence Place is the terrace forming the top end of the square; there the trees shade the pavement and the terraces are in good condition. They remind one of Bloomsbury, except for the wooden railings and privets of the gardens. There is also Clapton Mews, a local pub, and streets of small houses and shops, the whole once ministering to the requirements of the better-class houses in the square on a pattern familiar in Belgravia and other parts of the West End. Old photographs show how attractive Hackney once was as a residential area; today its former rural charm can only be guessed at. On each side Clapton Square rapidly shades off to Gothic terraces and gloomy blocks of flats.

Summer evening in
Clarence Place
Hackney

24

St. Paul's, Shadwell

———— ✳ ————

THE SEAMEN'S ST. PAUL'S, rebuilt in 1820 by a little-known architect, John Walters. The portico and steeple are very skilfully adjusted to form a subtle, harmonious arrangement. The interior of the church is restrained to the point of severity. St. Paul's is one of the most successful of the Waterloo churches and with its Institute and setting of a green and leafy churchyard forms an architectural composition in complete contrast to the surrounding streets and docks. The construction of the London Docks brought great changes to Shadwell. It ceased to be a place of residence for sea captains, and a new and increasing labouring population was crowded into poky houses thrown up in narrow alleys and courts. The captains and those who supplied the ships – instrument makers, ships' chandlers, sailmakers – departed from the Ratcliffe Highway and the neighbourhood degenerated still further with the coming of steam.

25

East End Junk Yard:
Sawing up the Queen's Music Hall

———————— ✳ ————————

'YOU'RE AFTER relics of the old Queen's Music Hall? Come in the yard and look round – no need ter buy. I've got masses of it. I'm sawin' up part of the bar nah; lovely stuff, teak and mahogany mostly. I remember the old place when it wus gas-lit. When I wus a young feller I had a crush on Gertie Gitana . . . oh, so you know 'er 'usband – well, I used to follow 'er around and jump on 'er car . . . wunce I took 'er pianist up the river to Canvey Island an' we got fog-bahnd and 'e missed the fust act. Those were the days – the old days. I'm 74 nah; used to take the old sailing barges full of coke to St. Valery before the 1914 war an' I can parley vous and sang froid with the rest. You'd like ter buy the notice wiv the 'and pointing to the gents, yes, sir, two bob, from the old Queen's what I'm sawin' up nah. Them two coats of arms is going to the Theatre Royal, Stratford, likewise the spiral staircase. . . . One belonged to King George III and the other to King Edward when 'e wos Prince of Wales. But I must be getting on with me work while yer look round. It makes good firewood, the old Queen's Music Hall.'

QUEENS

CURTAIN

STALLS

26

The 'Waterman's Arms'
Isle of Dogs

———— * ————

THE SPONTANEOUS public-house sing-song by a bunch of locals grouped round a piano topped with glasses is harder to find in the East End at the present time. Instead, music and gaiety are more self-consciously provided by the so-called music-hall pubs, where the entertainment, often of a raw description, is by professionals and would-be professionals, often on a stage. Real music-hall artistes such as Ida Barr appear, however, at the 'Waterman's Arms', once the 'Newcastle', in the Isle of Dogs. Here the public and saloon bars are separated by a low balcony, and there is a collection of old song covers, playbills and photographs of music-hall stars on the walls. Many of these music-hall souvenirs were originally in the bar of Collins', Islington; another relic is the caryatid figure from the vanished Metropolitan.

The next move is from the 'Waterman's Arms' to the 'City Arms', Millwall. The bar is crowded to suffocation on Saturday nights. The teenager patrons start to sway like reeds as a three-piece outfit opens up from its stage decorated with pop record sleeves. Middle-age couples appear bewildered by the whole thing. The 'City Arms' prefers various jocular announcements to line walls instead of the more staid music-hall items; a portrait of Cleopatra, for instance, who is represented as saying 'Everything I like is illegal, immoral and fattening' is typical of the rest. The dress (expensive and flashy) of the younger clients and their taste in booze is something to speculate upon in these East End pubs – to those who knew them in the dark ages.

HARRY TATE

TOM E. HEA
STAR CON

RUAPPING OLD STAIRS

BRITANNA
RICH

3 BROTHER OFFICERS

Watermans Arms
Isle of Dogs

27

Doric Road, Bethnal Green

———————— ✳ ————————

'Twas August, and the fierce sun overhead
Smote on the squalid streets of Bethnal Green,
And the pale weaver, through his windows seen
In Spitalfields, look'd thrice dispirited;

I met a preacher there I knew, and said:
'Ill and o'erworked, how fare you in this scene?'
'Bravely!' said he; 'for I of late have been
Much cheer'd with thoughts of Christ, the living bread.'

THE DRAWING is a typical Bethnal Green street of the period of Matthew Arnold's poem: it was formerly named Alma Road, which dates it accurately. The old vistas of the area are now increasingly dominated by great blocks of flats, but some of the master weavers' houses remain. Seabright Street provides good examples. These houses have large first-floor windows to the former workrooms. The silk weaving industry, now defunct, was brought to Spitalfields and Bethnal Green by the Huguenot refugees, who came here after the revocation of the Edict of Nantes. Some thirteen thousand settled in the East End in 1687. Almost the whole of Spitalfields was developed by them. The last traces of this once prosperous Huguenot community have been practically obliterated, except for family and street names.

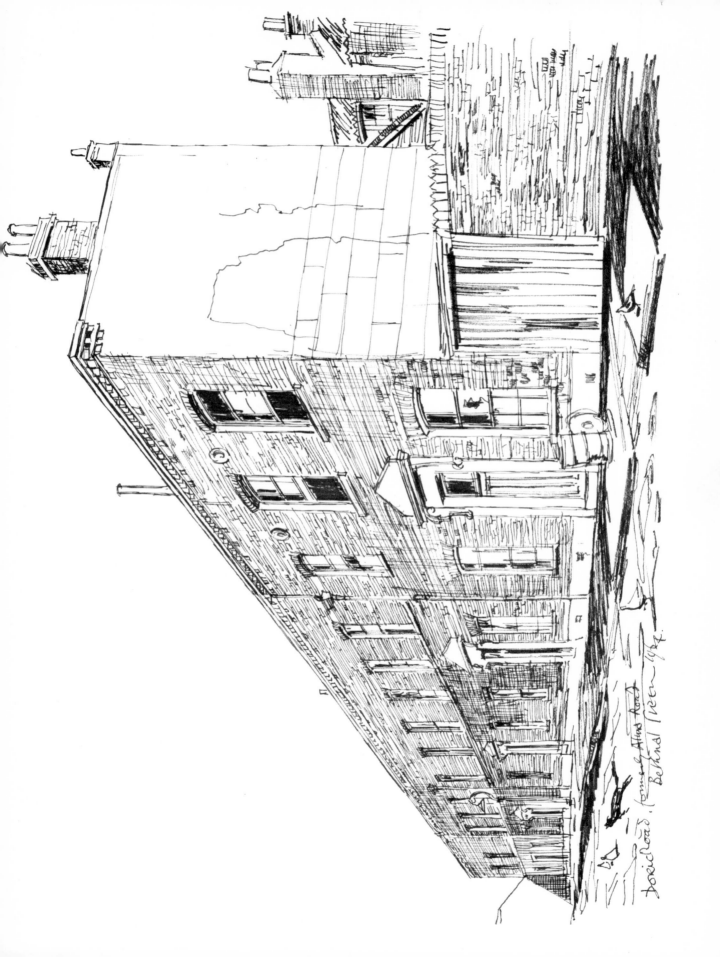

Doric Road. (formerly Atlas Road)
Bethnal Green 1987.

28

North-East Passage
Wellclose Square

———————— * ————————

WELLCLOSE SQUARE, with its early warehouses, seventeenth- and eighteenth-century buildings, court house and music hall, will soon belong to the past. North-East Passage connects the square to Cable Street; Grace's Alley, on the opposite corner of the square, commemorates the Cistercian Abbey of St. Mary of Graces, founded by Edward III, near to St. Katharine's Docks. The Regency house to the right of the drawing is worthy of St. John's Wood or Brighton. The Ionic pilasters are of fine quality, as is the cornice above with an egg and dart moulding. The stucco, furred with dirt, is peeling and crazed with neglect. The shop below is later, being cut into the original ground floor, part of which remains in a window. There are other good but worn-out houses – mainly of the eighteenth century – on this side of the square, with well-proportioned panelled rooms, all awaiting demolition.

29

Street Market, Deptford

———— * ————

DOUGLAS WAY, Deptford, Saturday morning. Stalls of pop records, animal foods, equipment for the modern budgie, dress and toy stalls, stalls for all the wants of mortal man.

''Ere yer are – luvly lettuces, two for a tanner, only a couple left. Luvly marrers – who wants a marrer for a tanner?' These 'luvly lettuces', however, were a combination of Art and Nature, for their dilapidated owner had assembled a collection of bruised, discarded specimens of unsavoury appearance, cut off the damaged parts, wrapped them in some blue paper cadged for the purpose and finally placed them in a box. Similar vendors can be seen operating in the *quartier* of St. Denis after the main business of Les Halles has been done by about 8 a.m., at which time come those who dodge up discarded fruit and vegetables: the very poor pick out the left-overs for themselves. As I drew, I noticed an old man (this is the lowest stage) helping himself to fruit out of the trailer parked by the Council's dustmen.

Note the stall of tapestries: highly coloured affairs they are too, the favourite subjects being 'The Stag at Bay', a ferocious lion and the Taj Mahal. Douglas Way is an El Dorado for the vintage record collector. On the day this drawing was made, I picked up a dozen music-hall records, all in good condition, including Billy Williams's 'My Ballooning Girl', each at a tanner. Who wants a marrer for a tanner?

Street Market. Deptford

30

Victorian Lamp, Bankside
Southwark

———————— ✳ ————————

IN PARK STREET and one of the finest in London. No one surely could be vandalistic enough ever to destroy it? One can never be sure in present-day London: already nasty new neighbours – concrete lamps of baleful aspect – have taken up threatening positions. This mid-nineteenth-century lamp is on a granite base, much worn. Its cast iron standard is of superb design and proportions. The early Victorians would have described it as elegant and chaste. The column is at present painted silver, though the paint has been knocked off in several places, disclosing thick layers of reddish paint below. In the background is the demolition of Barclay's old brewery, which is being replaced by a completely modern building.

DANGER
DEMOLITION

DANGER
DEMOLITION

DANGER
DEMOLITION

Park Street
Bankside Southwark

31

Limehouse Lock

———————— ✳ ————————

AN INCREDIBLE amount of human and animal life is somehow crowded into these British Waterways' cottages and the terrace in front of them, above the pea-green waters of Limehouse Lock. Dogs, kids and cats abound, the two last named being intrepid and venturesome, climbing like monkeys over the guard rails and along the parapet walls. One of these daring infants had met a watery end the week before this drawing was made. Lines of washing stretch from the canopies of the doors to posts by the lockside, and a picturesque touch is added by the traditional lock furniture – yellow and blue painted gates and flower tubs filled with geraniums in the summer. Limehouse Cut was one of the early canals, linking the Lea with the Thames in 1770 and foreshadowing the coming industrialisation of the East End.

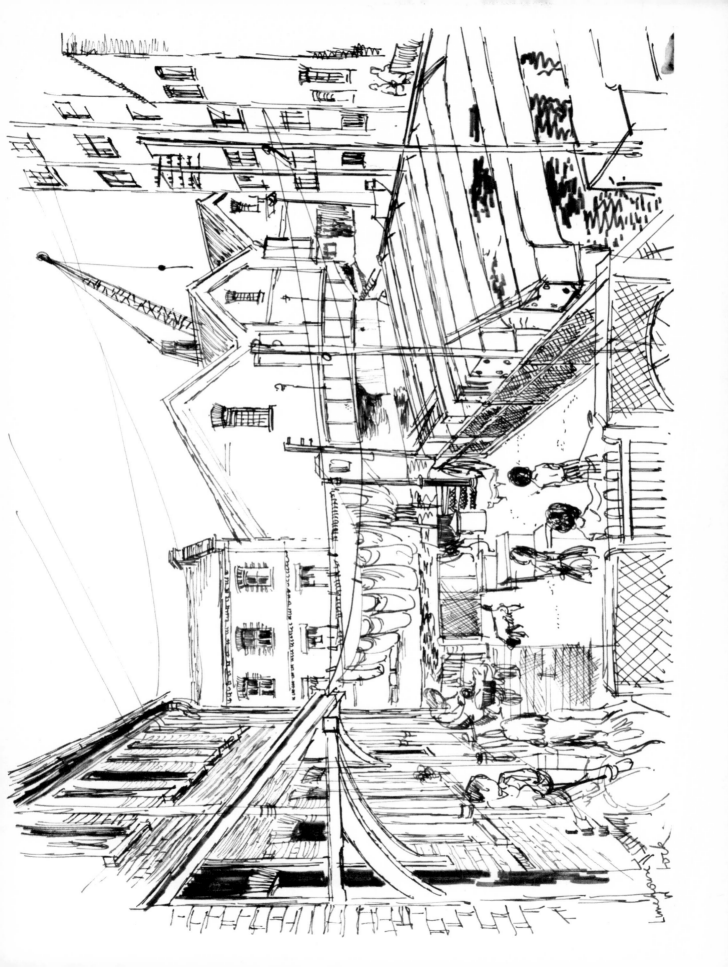

32

Hackney Empire:
Bingo Tonight and Every Night

———————— * ————————

HACKNEY IS a stimulating place of sick and burial societies, pram-pushing women and old men disconsolately sitting among privets. The Empire, built in 1901, is all but impossible to describe; it is a wonderful architectural nightmare with strange terra-cotta domes, apparently of Russian inspiration. It is a matter of infinite regret that architects have entirely lost the art of building in this un-inhibited manner. Red and yellow tiles remain in the entrances, and the Art Nouveau leaded lights to the side doors. The main doors still have their pretty oval glass panels with the engraved lettering 'Grand Circle' and 'Fauteuils', which reflect the Pavilion opposite as in a mirror. Behind the Empire there is a little bit of Georgian village architecture, including a group of almshouses, and the old 'Ship Inn', Victorian pub architecture at its confident best. Hackney Pavilion was opened in 1914. The entrance fee was a penny. The screen was in the centre, and late-comers had to sit behind it and see everything backwards.

33

Shop in Artillery Lane
Spitalfields

———— * ————

ONCE A silk merchant's shop and ascribed to Abraham Swan, a carpenter, who was the author of several builders' pattern books. The style is Roman Doric with rococo swags of fine quality above the shop door and above the door at the side, which gave access to the merchant's house above. It dates from *c.* 1750, the iron-work being later, and is without question the finest shop front in London still *in situ*. Considering the downtown nature of the area, the survival of the shop is a near miracle, but it is certainly not improving in appearance by continued sojourn there. The whole ought to be removed to the Victoria and Albert Museum for preservation. As it stands, the old shop is in constant danger, besides being an anachronism among the filthy Pakistanis, the evil-smelling white kids and derelict old men. Nuns stride past talking earnestly, rattling their beads, vacant girls walk about with transistors and old men roll up their trousers to apply ointment to scabby legs. Over all, a deafening noise from the betting shop in the odoriferous alley.

Artillery Lane.

34

Wentworth Street

————————— ✳ —————————

WENTWORTH STREET market is at its peak at midday. It is a place of fish, loud ties, handbags, transistors and blood-curdling oaths of lurid grandeur. There are also cages of fowls, whose crowing can be heard above the hoarse voices of the marketeers. All this restless movement, colour and clamour flows below the penitentiary-like blocks of Victorian dwellings that rise in massive cliffs above the crowd, a human river in a dirty grey canyon. My drawing was made from the corner of Leyden Street by the side of the lavatory, the attendant of which was raptly gazing at the market crowds from behind his own bars. Note the cast-iron street lamp which has an attractive medallion of the Tower on its plinth.

Wentworth Street

35

The Stones of Stepney:
Gothic in Glamis Road

———————— * ————————

A BOOK might be devoted to the Gothic of the East End, describing and analysing the romantic architecture that the Victorians injected into the mean jerry-built streets, no doubt in order that the costermongering and labouring classes might benefit from foliated capital, traceried window and pinnacled tower. It is impossible to decide whether they benefited or not, but it seems unlikely. There is a world of difference between looking through a cusped and mullioned window on to an Oxford quadrangle and through an identical window overlooking a soap works: only those with a special turn of mind could savour both equally. The iron railings in the foreground are those of the East London Hospital for Children, a decayed Gothic building of 1875, mostly in brick. Even more than most hospitals, it must have struck terror into its patients. There is a disused, crumbling drinking fountain by the entrance to the dispensary. The architectural ornament of the hospital is almost entirely confined to the entrance porch. In the distance is the spire of St. Mary's, Cable Street – conveniently situated with an undertaker's on the opposite side of the street.

The Stones of Stepney –
Sophie in Glamis Road

36

Priscilla Almshouses, Bow

——————— * ———————

THE FATE of this delightful group, once the Drapers' Almshouses, at the south end of Priscilla Road is still undecided. Their condition is deplorable, but they are not yet beyond rescue and restoration. They date from 1706. Almshouses were once common in the East End and survive now in reduced numbers as a reminder of the former rural character of the area. Bow was pleasantly countrified up to a late period: Dickens's readers will recall Mrs. Nickleby's pretty cottage there and her mad neighbour who threw cucumbers over her garden wall. The old houses in Bow Road are nearly all gone, apart from one or two near the church.

Many of these groups of almshouses were more or less in the style of Wren, who is traditionally associated with the design of the delightful Trinity Almshouses at Mile End, superbly restored by the L.C.C. The Priscilla Almshouses, although neither so well sited nor so ambitious, are in a similar manner and have fine carved brackets to the door of the central pedimented chapel.

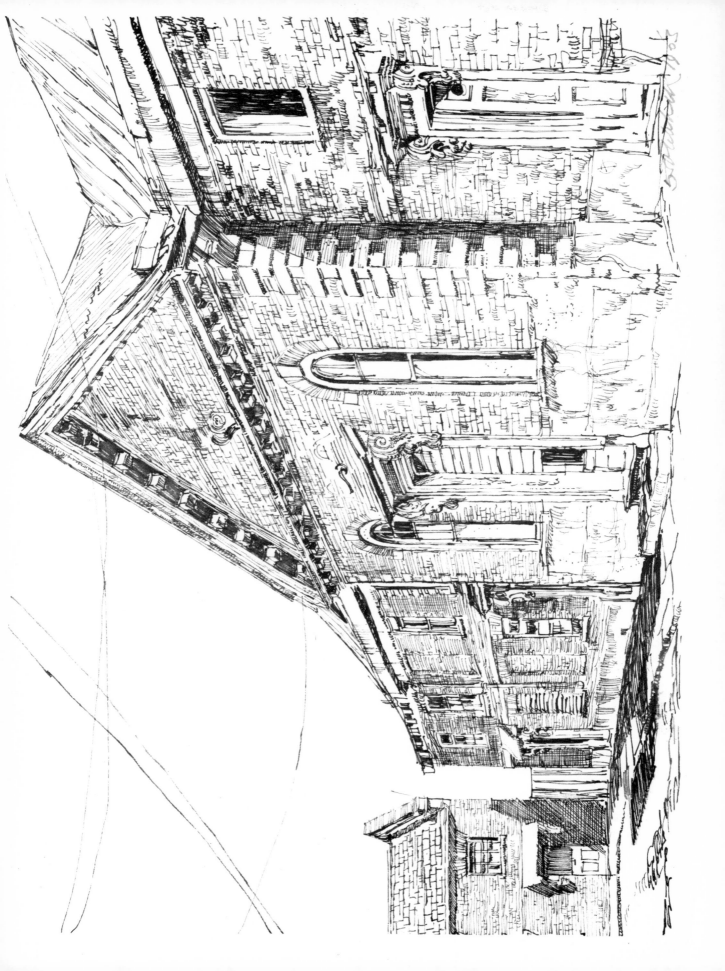

37

Cable Street, Stepney

———— * ————

CABLE STREET, like Basin Street, is where the white folk and dark folk meet: a blues singer would be much more likely to find material here than in Tin Pan Alley. Most of it is unredeemed, though there is a terrace of late Georgian houses close to Stepney Town Hall, some of which have their original shutters. This part of Cable Street is quite properly destined for early demolition. Left to itself, it would collapse of its own accord, for its decrepit houses are rotten with age and neglect. Cable Street is full of negro-haunted cafés, from which jazz oozes. Coloured men with money set up a type of lodging house run on a Box and Cox system. One set of inmates is given its exodus at 9 p.m. or 10 p.m. to make way for another set who occupy the same rooms and beds until morning. Those thrown out while away the night in Cable Street cafés or else lounge in the stinking, greasy alleys. West Enders are not unknown here. They come for drugs.

Cable Street

38

The 'Town of Ramsgate', Wapping

———————— ✳ ————————

IMMEDIATELY NEXT to Wapping Old Stairs, one of the many narrow alleyways from the High Street to the river, in a landscape of wharves and warehouses. On the right of the drawing is part of the attractive group of early nineteenth-century terraces by the old entrance to the London Docks. The inn has been modernised, but parts of it date from the seventeenth century. Before the railways, fishermen from Ramsgate came up the Thames to sell their fish in London, and they landed it at Wapping Old Stairs. The inn, originally called the 'Red Cow', was renamed in order to attract their custom. It was in the 'Town of Ramsgate' that Judge Jefferies, disguised as a common seaman, was captured after being recognised by a money-lender; an alarm was given and a mob at once surrounded the alehouse. Jefferies was rescued by the militia and died in the Tower from a wasting disease, ultimately being buried beneath the altar of St. Mary Aldermanbury, a Wren church now being dismantled for shipment to America. Macaulay gives a racy account of the incident.

39

Tanner's Hill, Deptford

————————— ✳ —————————

THIS GROUP of richly picturesque houses forms the oldest part of Deptford. They were once inhabited by tanners and leatherdressers, whose shops stretched up to the windmill. Today only a handful of ancient houses remains, the rest being Victorian: all are small businesses – greengrocers, fruiterers, newsagents and junk shops higher up the hill. In the triangle formed by Deptford Broadway and Tanner's Hill was once the Pound, where animals escaped from the neighbouring cattle market were kept. T. V. Cudbird, harnessmaker, who died in September 1964, aged over ninety, was the last of the leathermen, carrying on his trade to the end. The old cobbles are still underneath the modern concrete flags in the foreground pavement.

FRAMES HAND BUILT
ON THE PREMISES

WITCOMB

T.V. CUDBIRD   HARNESS MAKER   FINDUS   FINDUS   SUPPLIERS TO   REPAIRS   OLYMPIC
                                                      H.M. FORCES   ENAMELLING   OFFICIAL

Tinkers Hill
Deptford

40

Gents' Urinal, Limehouse

———— * ————

URINAL, DRINKING FOUNTAIN and gas lamp – all three under a grim railway arch: what could be better? Occasionally, a brewer's dray, drawn by two fine carthorses, unloads at a neighbouring pub; the arrangement is then quite perfect. Brick, tile or cement conveniences of this type are, of course, purely utilitarian and deficient in the artistic qualities found in those of cast iron; nonetheless they have character and interest, a sort of stark heroic quality, especially when topped by iron spikes. The East End is full of them, particularly in the streets bordering the river, both on the south and north sides.